MW00978907

The Marriage Challenge

Challenge

52 Conversations
for a better marriage

Andrea & James T. Wood

Cover image by Paul Fris, befresh.net

Author photo by Anni Becker
facebook.com/annibeckerphotography

This work is not intended to replace professional marriage or personal counseling or psychiatric help. Consult your mental health professional for additional help.

ISBN: 1494285517
ISBN-13: 978-1494285517

Dedication

Dr. Shawn Jones and Nancy Jones for starting us on the path to marriage enrichment.

Our Sycamore View Church small group, you taught us how to share and grow in our marriage.

The members of the 2010 Marriage Challenge, for pushing us to create this book.

     and

Breanna Newbill for taking comments on Facebook too seriously.

Acknowledgements

I don't have enough thanks to offer my tireless editor, Kathy McCurdy, who offered thoughtful advice and gentle correction without affecting the tone and style of the work. Those are rare talents, and even more rare to find in one person.

Much credit is due to the community of people who gathered around their computer screens and read the words of the 2010 Marriage Challenge as it went out (almost regularly) each week during that year. Together we learned how to be less terrible and a bit more awesome.

Thanks for the freely given critique of covers offered by my friends on Facebook. You deserve a share of the limelight – unless the book totally fails, then I'm blaming you.

Contents

Introduction to the Second Edition

We first published this book at the end of 2011 as a sort of experiment. We wanted to share what we've learned about marriage and I (James) wanted to learn about publishing and self-publishing.

Since then we've sold and given away thousands of copies of the book and continued to learn even more about marriage, both through our own experience and through learning from others. It's been fascinating, confusing, encouraging, depressing, fun, and scary to share our story with the world and offer some small bit of help for marriages and committed relationships over the last two years.

One of the most important things we've learned is that both healing and improving are important, but separate tasks. Some relationships need to heal, they've taken so many hits that they need time to work through all of the injuries and get back to a place of equilibrium and health. But marriages that are generally healthy don't need as much of the healing, but they do need more of the improving. The best analogy I've heard about this is that of the physical therapist and the personal trainer. Both are necessary jobs, but sending an injured person to a personal trainer won't help, nor will it do much good to send a healthy person to a physical therapist.

This book is intended to fill the role of a personal trainer. It's about taking healthy marriages and giving them the tools to become healthier. It's not about helping marriages that are hurting — there are plenty of other books for that. This repeats some ideas from the original introduction, but I'm okay with that. It's important enough to be said twice.

Another thing that we've learned over the last two years is that books take on a life of their own. This one did far more than I ever anticipated, but also fell short of what I hoped. I did several things wrong. This edition has been freshly edited, there are new sections and the language used throughout has been made consistent.

We've also learned that "marriage" is a word fraught with conflict from religious, social, and political perspectives. We have religious, social, and political ideas, but don't think they're really germane to a conversation about improving relationships. We keep the word "marriage" in the title and often use it throughout the book, but our intent is to encompass committed relationships, no matter what your social, political, or religious views are. Our thought is that instead of arguing over what defines a specific word, maybe we can do something to improve relationships, whatever they might be called.

Thank you for picking up — or downloading — this book. We hope it will challenge, encourage, enlighten, and motivate you to have the best relationship you can.

Introduction to the First Edition

Better marriages don't just happen, they take time and work. But you might be surprised at how much you can accomplish in just a little bit of time and with just a bit more effort. If you can make time in your schedule to have a one-hour conversation with your spouse every week, at the end of a year you can have a much better marriage.

Most marriages aren't in meltdown-crisis mode. Most marriages are pretty good; not perfect, but okay. Most marriage books, however, are written for people in crisis mode, about marriages that are falling apart and by counselors who only deal with failing relationships. Those books serve a good purpose, but they don't help the majority of marriages that aren't in that position yet.

This book isn't about how to fix all the stuff you're doing wrong. If you need that, you need a different book (and there are plenty of great options out there, check out the bibliography for some of our favorites). But, if you want to start with your marriage that's okay now and work to make it great, then this is the book you're looking for.

The challenge is this: have one conversation a week, every week for the next year. That's it. It will probably take about an hour of your life to read the short section for that week and talk through the questions that follow. The plan is to make it simple and painless. The sections average about three paragraphs and get to the point, then there are about three discussion topics, questions or conversation starters. You don't have to use the printed questions if you don't want to. They're just there to help you get into a conversation. If you only talk about the first question, that's fine, or if you blow through all the questions quickly and have a different conversation, that's great too.

The real goal of this book is to get you and your spouse into the habit of talking about your relationship. What's going to transform your marriage from "pretty good" into ""envy-of-the-neighbors amazing" is the consistent practice of communication. That's both speaking and listening (just in case you forgot).

Ready to get started?

Here are the rules:
1. Block out at least an hour to sit down and have these conversations. No distractions. No TV, no Internet, just the two of you talking.
2. Be consistent. Try to meet at the same time every week.
3. Have fun. Go on a coffee date or talk over a candle-lit dinner of mac and cheese.
4. No guilt. These conversations are for your benefit. If you miss one, just pick up where you left off. A one-year plus one -week challenge still gets you to a better marriage.

Ready?

Start by writing down a few things about your marriage. What are your major arguments? What makes you happy? What do you never expect to change? What hopes do you have for the future of your marriage?

Hold on to this paper for a year. At the end of the Marriage Challenge compare your thoughts then and now to see the progress you've made in your marriage.

Communication

Good communication is the foundation of a great marriage. How we share, encourage, criticize and disagree has a profound impact on the state and health of our marriage. Since without communication, the rest of this book is useless, we're going to start with some principles for how to communicate well. As with everything that you read, apply this to your life and your marriage. Andrea and I have learned a lot and read a lot about marriage, but we've never had your marriage. You are the experts in that field. Your communication styles will affect everything else. Take a moment, before you have your first conversation, and think about how you communicate. Are you typically argumentative? Do you avoid conflict? Do you make jokes when you're nervous? What helps you communicate and what makes it difficult for you to get your point across?

Week 1 – Safe Place

Early on in our marriage we learned the concept of the "safe place" which says that we should assume our spouse intended to be nice rather than mean. Too often we assume the worst about our spouse – they didn't do the dishes because they're a jerk; they intentionally deleted the football game to get back at me for not doing the dishes; they broke my porcelain unicorn riding a rainbow because they think it looks ridiculous. What if we assume the nicest thing first? We assume that the dishes were an oversight, the football game deletion was an accident, and the unicorn destruction was an act of mercy (kidding). The odds are good that the person who married you because they love you, is not out to be a jerk to you. Give them the benefit of the doubt.

Get to know how your communication might be understood or misunderstood and then put that information to work before you speak. Andrea and I have discovered that there are certain things that could be taken in both a good way and a bad way. We came up with the phrase: "Take this how I mean it," as a preface to something that could have two meanings. For example: "You look terrible!" Could mean that your spouse needs to put a paper bag over their head (the bad meaning) or that you are super sensitive and noticed they had a bad day at work (the good meaning). If you take fifteen seconds, before you open your mouth, to think about how your words might come across, you can avoid a lot of arguments before they even happen.

Discussion:

Discuss a time where you assumed the wrong meaning for something. How did it turn out? How long did it take you to figure out the correct meaning and resolve the issue?

Share an experience where your meaning was misunderstood. How did you feel? How did that affect your ability to move forward?

What one topic or area of your marriage has made you feel the most misunderstood in the last month? Why?

How could you communicate in order to be better understood?

How could you better understand your spouse?

Week 2 – Watch Your Language

The language we use is incredibly important in our communication. We may have the best intentions in mind, but if the words we use don't reflect those intentions, then all sorts of bad stuff can happen. So, watch your language. This isn't just about cuss words, but about any words (or tones) that might be hurtful or offensive to your spouse.

One classic example is to use "I feel" statements when you express an opinion. Saying: "You don't care about me," can be hurtful since it casts blame on your spouse and makes the statement general instead of specific. Rather, you could say: "When you cook salmon for dinner, I feel hurt, like my preferences don't matter." That makes the statement specific and about the situation and keeps it about the feelings of the person speaking.

The goal is honesty with tact, both truth and love. You don't want to lie to your spouse and tell them that you love salmon when you hate it. You also don't want to be rude and hurtful to your spouse in response because that will just escalate things (you feel hurt so you hurt them in retaliation). Instead, take a moment to pause and re-frame your thoughts with more tact.

Marriage is an incredibly vulnerable place. This other person knows more about you than just about anyone else in the world. They have the ability to say things that will cut through to the core of your soul. That vulnerability is the path to an amazing, deep, rewarding, fulfilling relationship, but it's a risk as well.

Discussion:

Relational culture is the specific language that you and your spouse have with each other. Talk about some aspects of your own relational culture. What's unique to the two of you? What communication would only you understand?

Ask your spouse about a time when they said something hurtful to you. Practice using "I feel" statements. Be careful to not get defensive here, the goal is to just share experiences, not to cast blame.

Week 3 – Getting to Yes

The book *Getting to Yes* is all about how to negotiate, so it's a perfect fit for a marriage discussion. The truth is that marriage involves daily negotiation and if you try to negotiate with your spouse like you would with a used car salesperson, you will always have a loser in the relationship. *Getting to Yes* focuses on four principles that can lead to win-win negotiation.

1. *Separate the people from the problem*
    This means that you don't view your spouse as the source of the problem, but that the problem is external to your relationship. Sometimes we even sit on the same side of a table just for the physical symbolism that we are united against a problem.

2. *Focus on interests, not positions*
    Positions are what we say we want, interests are what we actually want. Usually positions are difficult to negotiate, but you can have interests in common. She wants to go shopping and you want to go watch the game – those are positions that are in conflict. But if you dig to the interests you might find that you both just want some time away from the house.

3. *Invent options for mutual gain*
    Here's where you can get creative. Once you know your interests you have a better chance of finding a solution to the problem that satisfies both of your interests. You can both win in this negotiation.

4.   *Insist on using objective criteria*
This one can be a little different in marriage, but it's still very possible. The book talks about using a salary survey to discuss your raise and other examples from the business world. But we've found it to be helpful to use real dollar amounts and real times when talking about things – such as, I need $25 for the class or, we can spend 10 minutes in this store. We even use a scale of 1 to 10 to discuss how much we want to attend a certain event.

Andrea & James T. Wood

Discussion:

Discuss a time when you've negotiated with someone else. What tactics did you use?

Where did you learn to negotiate? How does that come into play in your marriage?

Is there often a winner and a loser in your conflict? How does that make you feel?

Week 4 –
Listening/Assumptiveness

One of the really great things about being married is having someone who knows you better than anyone else in the whole world. They can finish your sentences and know what you want for dessert before you do. One of the infuriating things about marriage is having someone who thinks they know you better than you know yourself. They are constantly trying to put words in your mouth and won't even let you finish a sentence and maybe you actually wanted cake tonight.

Even though it's not really a word, we've been calling this assumptiveness. The state of being assumptive.

It's a problem for us to assume what our spouse wants, but it's also a problem when we don't get specific and say what we want. You can't blame your spouse for making assumptions when you don't offer any alternatives. If you have something specific that you want to happen, say it. Specifically. As well as your spouse knows you and you know them, neither one of you can read minds. Kill assumptiveness with specificity.

Andrea & James T. Wood

Discussion:

Imagine you got an extra $100 and so did your spouse. Write down what you think your spouse would buy with the money. Then compare notes.

Discuss why you assumed your spouse's purchase. Why were you right/wrong?

Sometimes it's nice when we can assume that our spouse will think/do something. It's great when I can just ask Andrea to order something for me and I'm sure that I will like it because she knows what I like. Discuss a time when you have really enjoyed assumptiveness in your marriage.

But, other times being vague and assumptive can be frustrating. What makes the difference? What habits could you start that would encourage good assumptiveness and discourage frustration?

Romance

Romance may or may not be important to you, but chances are your spouse would like some of it. It's difficult to define exactly what is romantic since it's different for every person and every couple. But, when you work together to find ways to express your love, it will strengthen every aspect of your marriage.

Week 5 – 5 Love Languages

The book *The 5 Love Languages* by Gary Chapman shares the secret that we all want to be loved, but we speak different love languages. So when I'm trying to communicate to Andrea that I love her, I'm going to default to my own love language and if that's not her love language, she won't get what I'm trying to communicate. This is why sometimes one spouse can be working constantly and end up frustrating their partner who just wants to spend some time together. Or when one partner gets a generic gift for their spouse and walks headlong into a fight for their trouble. They're speaking different love languages.

The languages are: Acts of Service, Gifts, Meaningful Touch, Words of Affirmation, and Quality Time. The workaholic spouse thinks that they're expressing love for their through his service, but their partner just wants some quality time. The spouse wants a gift that is meaningful, but his partner communicates love through hugs and touches. Some people just need to hear that they are loved with affirming words.

I find myself trying to sooth my wife by doing the dishes or making the bed, but my acts of service are mostly lost when she just wants a hug. Andrea will try to love me by spending some quality time, but I just want to hear that she's proud of me. When we communicate love in our own languages, the message is often lost. But when we work to learn the language of our spouse, we can target our love messages to them and we can better receive the love that they are sending our way.

Discussion:

Write down what you think your love language(s) are and then write down what you think your spouse's love language(s) are. Then, before you tell each other what you wrote, go to 5lovelanguages.com and take the quiz to find out what your love languages really are. Then compare. Talk about why you were right or wrong with your guess about yourself. Talk about why you were right or wrong with your guess about your spouse.

Ask your spouse about one or two ways that you can speak and listen to their love language(s). Be specific. If your love language is meaningful touch, don't just say: "Touch me." Instead say: "Rub my shoulders when I get home from work."

Note: you can have more than one love language. For this week try to focus on your top language and your spouse's top language. But, because you're incredibly talented and capable, you will be able to branch out to the next language very soon.

Week 6 – Special Events

Special events can cause some special moments in marriage. But often they cause very special fights. We're coming up on one of the most famous, or infamous depending on your perspective. There's a lot that goes into our special event arguments. So we're going to break it down a little bit.

Counselors like to use the term "family of origin" to talk about some of these issues. Basically what you need to figure out is the effect your upbringing has on your marriage. Guess what. It's a lot. The way that your family celebrated holidays, gave gifts, and showed affection are all floating around in your head making it difficult for your spouse to celebrate a special day with you.

Also, remember the love languages (from last week). Here's a huge application. Do you get flowers for Valentine's Day or not? What is your spouse's love language? That will tell you how they want to be loved. Some days are very focused on gift giving (birthdays or Christmas) which can be tough on someone who doesn't have gifting as a love language. Help each other out here.

Finally, treat the disease not the symptom. When we were talking about this, Andrea kept thinking about the song: "I Want You to Want Me" as being very expressive of how she feels. She didn't want me to ask about the specific gift, but to know what she wanted. It's easy to just see the "symptom" of needing to get a gift for a special event, but that's not the place to focus. Instead we should focus on the "disease" of our spouses wanting to be known and loved. It's not really about the gift; it's about what the gift communicates.

Discussion:

Spend some time sharing with each other about your family of origin and how you celebrated holidays growing up. What differences are there? How do you think that is affecting what you do now?

Recap your love language conversation from last week. Remind each other what your language(s) are. One really good thing is to look for overlap – the language that you have in common that is highest for both of you (like meaningful touch for Andrea is "1"" and for me it's "3" so we share that language more than any other).

Tell a story about a past special event that has been just awful and why it was so bad (pick one you can laugh about – if it's still too soon, you should wait). Now tell a story about one of your favorite special events and what made it so good. What can you do to create more favorite moments?

Week 7 – Date Night

We've covered the special events that often trip us up, but what about the regular dating? Do you have a regular date night with your spouse? If so, good, that's a great practice. If not, maybe we can convince you to change your mind.

We can't figure out who first told us to keep dating, because so many people told us to keep dating. Before we were married we heard this advice so many times that we were half afraid to not take it. The principle is fairly simple – what got you to the point of wanting to be married is dating, so keep dating so you will keep wanting to be married. Simple, in theory.

Except that life often gets in the way. It's hard to get motivated to go out on a date when you have to work the next day or when you have to find a sitter for the kids or when you don't have any money in the budget. There are a lot of obstacles to dating as a married couple -- but it's worth it to get over them.

Sometimes our dates are very simple – Netflix and popcorn on the couch. Sometimes we get creative and go to the farmers' market to discover what we will have for dinner. Other times we're boring and go to a movie or out to dinner. But we try to date once a week (and we've been consistent over ten years of marriage with only a handful of misses).

Note: we date weekly, but we don't have kids – if you have kids you might only be able to do once or twice a month. But you need to date. Work out a babysitting swap with another couple your age or use the money you would spend on dinner to pay for a sitter and go to the park and sit on a blanket together.

When you're dating, be intentional and present. We've learned that sitting next to each other on the couch and watching a movie can be a good date time – if we both know it's a date and we're present with each other. During date time we don't get on our phones or computers. We don't talk about work or money.

Discussion:

Talk about the dates that you've been on with your spouse – come up with a list of your all-time, top five dates.

Spend some time talking about what life was like before you got married. What did you look forward to in your dates? Try to figure out what it was about your dates that was so attractive to the both of you? Was it adventure, discovery, companionship, or something else? How could you have dates now that capture the same spirit? Example: if you loved discovering new things together maybe you could take a pottery class.

Set some guidelines for what you want your dates to look like. Talk about a budget for dates and how often you think you can date. These don't have to be set in stone, but it will be helpful if you have similar expectations for your dates.

Week 8 – Sex

Sex is a natural, beautiful, amazing, intimate expression of love that needs to be celebrated and discussed. Sex is not naughty or evil or sinful or shameful. But since many of us have heard that message all our lives, we have some deprogramming to do. Sex is good. You are allowed to like sex. You are allowed to talk about sex. You are allowed to enjoy sex. The thing is that if you don't talk about it, it won't ever get any better.

Married sex is fantastic because you are with someone who sees you at your most awkward, confused, embarrassed and messed up and they still love you and want to see you the next day. Here's the thing – you need to talk about sex. There is no other way to get better at sex than talking about it. Talk about what works and what doesn't. Talk about what was too silly and what felt good. Talk about the frequency of sex and how long each encounter lasts. Talk about foreplay and when foreplay needs to start.

Experiment. Learn from trial and error (and there will be lots and lots of error). Share your fantasies and your fears. Talk about your history and your assumptions. If sex is awkward, talking about sex is a hundred times more awkward. It is just so weird to get done and cuddle up together and have a frank conversation about parts and positions. Get over it. Do it anyway. The results are so worth it. If you take time to talk about sex and to share with each other, then your sex life will get better and better. Imagine being 40 and having better sex than when you were 30 or 20. What about being 50 or 60?

Andrea & James T. Wood

Communication only makes it better. It's up to you.

Discussion:

It might be a good idea to have this conversation at night in bed with the lights out. For some reason it's easier to say all the intimate things when the lights are out and you aren't looking at each other. Find something that works for you to make these conversations happen. Please, please don't avoid this.

What are your favorite things about your sex life? What things get you excited about sex?

If you could change one thing about your sex life, what would it be? Why? Note: you can't change anyone but yourself – this is about how you can improve, not what your spouse needs to change.

Getting to Know Each Other

While communication is one of the most important aspects of a healthy relationship, one less well known aspects is knowing your spouse. It's an easy thing to assume, but it's more difficult to actually pull off. Sure you're married or in a deeply committed relationship, but there's always more that you can learn about your partner, if you're willing to put in the effort.

Week 9 – Preferences

What you like and what you don't like may not be the deepest level of your psyche, but it's an incredibly important part of knowing and being known by another person. Sure your favorite color, flavor of ice cream, or ideal band name may not affect most of the things you do on a daily basis, but having someone who knows those things can affect the quality and longevity of your relationship.

This is another one of those areas where it's not the thing, but it's the thought that counts. It doesn't matter so much that Andrea and I talk to each other in movie quotes (60% of the time), what does matter is that we do it for each other. I've written several books now, and in each of them there's a joke or reference that only Andrea will get. It's a way to communicate that I *know* her, not just about her, but I know her.

You may not communicate in movie quotes, that's probably a good thing. But the more time you spend learning about each other, what your partner likes and doesn't like, the more connected you'll feel and the stronger your relationship will be.

Discussion:

What do you know about each other that no one else does? How does it feel to be known that way?

Talk about a time you wished your spouse had known something about you but didn't. Why do you remember that moment?

What plans can you make to learn more about each other? What activity could you share this week that would help?

Week 10 – Personality Part 1

Since the time of Aristotle (and probably even earlier) people have been trying to figure out what makes people different. Aristotle came up with the four humors, thinking that there were four different liquids that flowed through people's bodies and, as such, gave their influence to different personality styles. He called the humors: melancholic, sanguine, phlegmatic, and choleric. Over the last 2300 years the names have changed, but the basic ideas have stayed the same.

Sanguine — This is the person who's the life of the party. They never get enough of being with people and people never seem to get enough of being with them. When things are going well it's a pleasure to be around them, but when conflict arises or jobs need to get done, they can be hard to find. They want to maintain the fun and can have a difficult time settling down to get work done or processing through conflict.

Choleric — This is the person who tells everyone to get to the party on time and play the games planned. They are the outgoing organizers the like to get things done. They often find themselves in leadership roles, in part, because they think no one else can do the job better than they can. They can be dominating and intimidating to other personalities. When things go poorly they can become frustrated. In conflict they tend to pursue and look for a way to win what they perceive as a battle.

Melancholic — This is the person who sits back at the party and observes everyone so they can journal about it all later. They are task-oriented, so if they show up to the party, they'd rather be keeping the buffet table filled than talking to people. They are excellent planners, but take time to consider all the possibilities so they can be frustrating to the Sanguine and Choleric types. In conflict they will avoid direct confrontation, but look for the best solution if given enough time and space. When things go poorly they will often shut down and be silent.

Phlegmatic — This is the person who is always near the life of the party. They don't need to be the center of attention, but they want to be at the center of the action. They love people, are extremely loyal, and want everyone to get along. They enjoy following much more than leading, especially if their leader is clear and kind. When things go poorly they tend to internalize conflict. They have a slow burn where it takes a long time to make them angry, but when they are they're very angry. The exception is if you hurt someone they care about, then the momma bear loyalty comes out as they seek to protect the people they love.

Most likely you are a combination of two or more of the personality types. These are considered to be the basic personality types which combine to create the complex, unique personalities that each individual has.

Andrea & James T. Wood

Discussion:

What personality type would you guess your spouse is? Why?

These personalities are the basic building blocks, but each person has a little of all the personality types. What do you think are your top two? Why is that?

What in your relationship could be explained by these personality types?

Week 11 – Personality Part 2

Personalities are complex (or had you noticed that already?) so a four-personality system might leave some people out. Whether the Aristotelian system makes sense to you, or something else does, the important thing is to find a tool that can help you to describe yourself to your spouse *and* can help you understand your spouse's point of view.

DiSC Profile - This is basically an update of the old-school personalities with names that are easier to understand (phlegmatic always makes me think of a person with a terrible head cold). D is for Dominant and is the same as Choleric; I is for Influence and corresponds with the Sanguine, S is for Steady and is the Phlegmatic. C is for Contemplative and lines up with the Melancholic. What the DiSC profile adds is some tools for figuring out which type you are — if you aren't certain — and interpreting the results.

Myers-Briggs Type Indicator — This is often abbreviated at MBTI, which is fitting since all the personalities are also combinations for four letters. This personality tool looks at four spectra and figures out how those four combine to create a personality. You can be Introverted or Extroverted, Sensing or Intuitive, Thinking or Feeling, and Judging or Perceiving. So I end up being classified as an INTJ because I'm Introverted, Intuitive, Thinking and Judging. Andrea is an ENSP because she's Extroverted, Intuitive, Sensing and Feeling. Overall this gives 16 different personality types that can explain how and why you are the way you are.

Andrea & James T. Wood

Enneagram — The Enneagram is based on systems theories and so tries to look at how personalities function within a system. There are nine personality types and, within each one, are different tendencies to move toward other behaviors when things are going well or when they're stressful. One is the Reformer a rational and idealistic person. Two is the Helper who cares for people. Three is the Achiever, always focused on success. Four is the Individualist who wants to stay alone. Five is the Investigator who is skeptical and thoughtful. Six is the Loyalist who remains committed to people and causes. Seven is the Enthusiast who cheers on friends. Eight is the Challenger who gets things done and doesn't take 'no' for an answer. Nine is the Peacemaker who brings everyone together.

Whichever personality survey works for you, the important thing is finding a tool to help understand yourself and your spouse. Some people feel no connection to one of the personality models, but another resonates with them strongly. Look at all the options and pick one (or two, or all three) that help you communicate better.

Discussion:

What did you learn from taking a personality survey that you hadn't thought of before? About yourself? About your spouse?

Where did the personality surveys fall short? What about you do they not cover? About your spouse?

How can you use a better understanding of your personality to communicate with your spouse? How do you think this might hinder communication?

Week 12 – Passions

Preferences and personality can say a lot about the "what" of your relationship, but passion speaks to the "why." Passion is why you get up in the morning and stay up late at night (other than coffee). Knowing the passions of your spouse can help you to understand and empathize with them in ways that other knowledge can't. Passion is also an integral part of purpose. When your career counselor in high school asked you the stock question: If you had a million dollars, what would you do with it? That was meant to get you thinking about what your passions are. The supposed answer to that question is what you should do for your career. Unfortunately most people can't make a career out of buying and consuming the largest red velvet (with cream cheese frosting) cake ever – that's what I would if I had a million dollars.

The underlying idea of the million-dollar-question is what you would choose to do, if you didn't have to earn a living. That gives some insight into what really drives you at a core level and helps to reveal why you make some of the choices you make. Also when our passions are thwarted, we can become grumpy, angry, or even depressed. We all want to feel like our lives have meaning, so when it doesn't feel that way it's not much fun.

Sharing passions is nice, but not absolutely necessary for a successful relationship. What is necessary is that each person has space for their passions without discounting or denigrating the passions of the other person. Andrea and I get to share our passion for music by being in a choir together, but we each have our own separate passions too. She doesn't really care about sports, but she supports me by giving me time to watch games. I don't really care about her crafting activities, but I'm happy to give her space to do them. Having shared passions and recognizing separate passions gives you the ability to affirm and support what's important to each of you without taking away what makes you a unique individual.

Andrea & James T. Wood

Discussion:

What was (or is) your answer to the million-dollar-question? Does that identify your passion? Why or why not?

What passions do you share or would you like to share? What do you need to do to make that happen?

What passions do you not share? How can you give each other space for those activities?

Support

We need help and we need to be helpers. This is especially true in a marriage relationship. This month we will explore how we can be good helpers and accept help well. The first week we'll talk about how to be supportive in a practical way, the next week we'll discuss how to support emotionally. The week after that we'll talk about appropriate ways to receive support from outside your marriage, and finally what to do when you are both stressed and need support at the same time.

Week 13 – How to be Supportive Practically

One of the beautiful things about being married is that we don't have to live life alone. When things get difficult, someone is there to stand with you and help you though. That's the idea, anyway. We need to support each other through life. It's part of that whole "sickness and health" thing that you promised.

Step one, pay attention to what your spouse is doing. Be aware of what they have on their plate and when it might get overwhelming. Use questions like: "How are you handling this?" or "Is there anything I can do to help?" Your goal is to look for things that might be raising stress in your spouse.

Step two, look for things that will specifically and actively help your spouse through this situation. Think of it in terms of reducing and removing stressors from their life. You can't do their homework for them, but you could make dinner while they focus on school. But make sure that you are relieving a stressor that they actually have: if Andrea offered to make the bed for me, it wouldn't matter to me too much because I'm not the one who cares if the bed is made. The same is true if I offered to update all the software on the computers – not a big deal for her.

Step three, overtly offer specific help to support your spouse. This will seem awkward at first to say something like: "I'm going to do the dishes to support you while you do your homework." But it's important to establish what you're doing and why you're doing it. Maybe the dishes will be a huge help, and maybe they won't – you will never know if you don't talk about it.

Don't rob your spouse of an opportunity to serve and love you. You may be tough and able to handle all the stress coming your way, but your spouse loves you and wants to help you. Here's where it can get difficult; ask for help. Recognize that you have a lot of stressors weighing on you right now and ask for help.

Andrea & James T. Wood

Discussion:

Share a time that you felt supported. What made you feel that way?

How have you asked for support in the past? Did that work well or poorly? What changes could you make to how you ask for support?

Make sneaky-ninja plans to support your spouse this week.

Week 14 – How to be Supportive Emotionally

Sometimes, it's not just the stuff that needs to get done. Sometimes, it's how we feel about the stuff that is the most important thing. We can support and be supportive in getting the dishes done or the bed made, but that doesn't address the emotional issues lying under the surface. Sure, beds and dishes aren't usually rife with deep emotional trauma, but work with me here.

You may have noticed last week that we differentiated between stress and stressors. That's some of my fancy, counseling learning coming out. Basically stressors are things that are external to us and stress is the response we have to stressors. It's important to differentiate because we need to know what we can change. To some degree we can choose our stress response – we can decide if we will let the broken transmission cause a meltdown or a belly-laugh. We can also work on eliminating stressors to some degree.

As the emotionally supportive spouse you need to remember that you can't change your spouse's stress response. You can't make them or keep them from feeling anything. You can do your best to remove stressors, which is good, but your spouse is responsible for their own emotions. If they agree, you can suggest some stress reduction techniques, but you cannot change what they are feeling.

There are a few techniques that we have found helpful for us (your results may vary). Sometimes a long, full hug is just the thing we need. I know this sounds like an after-school special, but just hugging helps – usually we're talking about a 30 second-plus, non-sexual hug. If you have a pet, snuggle with your pet – they are great at offering warmth and acceptance and they rarely get stressed. Also, sometimes you just need to get away – maybe for an hour or a weekend, but help each other to see when it's time to get out for a bit. Finally, sex can be a great stress relief. I wouldn't use sex like a prescription for Prozac, but sometimes it's a great way to reset the brain chemistry and reconnect with your spouse and to remember that the stressors in life just aren't that important.

Discussion:

What stressors really know how to push your buttons? Why do you think they get a higher stress response than other things? Is your stress response out of whack with what the stressors deserve?

Think about a time when you were very stressed and something calmed you down. What was it? Could you communicate that calming influence to your spouse?

What tips do you have for reducing stress and helping your spouse?

Week 15 – Outside Support

Your spouse can't meet all your needs. I hate to break it to you, but they can't. They may be the best person you've ever met, but they just can't do everything. If you put that kind of pressure on them and on the relationship you are setting both of you up for failure.

Sometimes when the stress gets too high you need to spend some time with other people. Having some good friends that are also married is a great way to do this. If you have friends that are going through the same things as you are (starting a career, having kids, buying a house, etc.) you can commiserate about what's happening in your life. It's also good to have a married couple in your life that is older; they can help guide you through some of this stuff because they've done it before. They won't replace your peers, but they are an amazing blessing.

Spend time away from your spouse. Go out with just your friends. Do stuff that your spouse isn't interested in doing — I'll have video game night with some friends, for example. Here's the important part, you can share stress, but don't vilify your spouse to your friends. Instead of saying: "My wife is so dumb, she spent all our money." Say something like: "We're really struggling with money right now." Obviously, sometimes your spouse is a stressor in your life, that's okay, and it's okay to share with your friends, but do your best to keep it positive. It helps nothing to have spouse bashing sessions. Keep it positive.

There are times when you can't do it on your own and

friends aren't cutting it. Guess what, there are professionals who can help you. There are marriage counselors who have gone to school to learn how to help you. There are support groups that are designed for just your issue. If you've tried to work through stuff on your own, ask for some help. It's really worth it.

Andrea & James T. Wood

Discussion:

What resources do you already have available to you that could provide support? Why are you not using them (if you aren't)?

Think of a time when your spouse has not understood what you're going through. What did you end up doing? Did you seek someone else? Why or why not?

Why do you think our culture tends to look down on those who receive professional support? Is this view accurate? Do you share this view?

Week 16 – What to do When You Both Need Support

Sometimes things work out so that you both need support at exactly the same time. Usually this is when you are both experiencing the same stressor at the same time. Moving, the death of a loved one, job loss, major illness – all sorts of things can cause a situation where you both need support at the same time. So, what do you do?

One thing you can do is to take turns giving and receiving support. This isn't a long-term solution, but it can get you through the immediate crisis. When Andrea's dad died I was pretty broken up by it, but I put my feelings aside to help her get through the roughest part. The problem is that when the crisis is past you can forget to let the other person have a turn. By the time I was ready to deal with my grief, the immediacy was gone and it felt awkward. We learned that it's important to take turns supporting each other. Even if it's awkward, it's necessary. Guys, you aren't tough enough to just take it and keep going. Don't try to be.

If ever there was a time to ask for help from friends and professionals, this is it. When you are both hurting and stressed you need support from someone else. I know it may not seem like it, but they will understand. I've been in the situation where I feel like my stuff is too trivial to bother anyone with, but it's big to me. Your friends will get it and they will support you through it.

Ultimately, the best salve is time. Take the time to work through this stuff. Take the time to support each other and to ask friends and professionals for help. But it won't be fixed overnight. You may have noticed the word 'through" showing up a lot this week – that's because you can't hide from this stuff. The only way out is through. Time won't help, professionals won't help, and friends won't help, if you aren't willing to deal with the issues. You might need to get away from it all – get a room somewhere far away from your life and just talk about things. Give yourself permission to work on things.

Discussion:

What does it look like when you both need support? What types of situations have you dealt with in the past?

What has made you feel better in past situations? Was it a short-term or long-term fix?

What needs to happen to move from a short-term fix to a long-term fix? What has worked for you to get out of crisis mode?

Week 17 – Support and Boundaries

We've touched on this a bit while talking about how we can support each other through stressful times, but this needs to be said explicitly. You need to have good boundaries in place in your marriage before stress comes so that you can come through the stress together. This week we'll touch on a couple of boundaries that are especially important during stress and then next month we'll look at more boundary issues.

Don't badmouth your spouse. It's tempting when you're stressed, but don't do it. Now sometimes your spouse is one of the stressors you are dealing with, sometimes you need to vent to someone about your frustration. If you have one or two close friends (that you aren't romantically attracted to) who know that you love your spouse and you're committed to your marriage, you can talk to them about your frustrations. Really the key here is to not have a bunch of people sitting around talking about how terrible their spouse is. In public you should only build up your spouse and praise them. If you do have some gripes, keep that between you and your closest friends with the understanding that you are venting so that you can work on your marriage.

Don't get support from someone who could be sexually attracted to you or that you might be sexually attracted to them. Sharing stressful situations is close, intimate stuff. There can be no confusion here, especially if you are sharing about your frustrations with your spouse. It would be a very bad idea to tell someone who is sexually attracted to you about how your spouse is frustrating you right now – they won't have your best interest in mind, but rather their attraction.

Finally, don't get support from your family (especially your parents) if your main stressor is your spouse. Parents have a hard enough time accepting the son or daughter-in-law; don't give them a reason to dislike the addition to the family. They will automatically take the side of their own child and usually will hold a grudge against the in-law child. If you are just venting a momentary frustration you can sour a life-long relationship between in-laws. Keep your conversation about your marriage positive in front of your parents and family.

Andrea & James T. Wood

Discussion:

What boundaries have you set in your marriage that are helpful for you?

Are there times when you didn't have boundaries in place that you wish you did? What happened? What would have changed with some boundaries in place?

What questions do you have about boundaries?

Boundaries

Having healthy, appropriate boundaries in place is a huge part of protecting your marriage. It's like having a fence around your garden to keep the deer out so that your vegetables can grow. Boundaries are not supposed to limit growth, but to provide a safe environment to promote growth.

Week 18 – Boundaries with Communication

A couple times we've mentioned these principles, but it's time to have a discussion about the boundaries in communication. What do we say, when do we say it, and to whom do we say it? This is important because there are all sorts of forces that will try to tear apart your marriage. Think of them like the critters that want to eat your garden. You need to protect against the big, obvious ones just as much as you need to protect against the tiny, insidious ones. Also, these are boundaries that we have learned – they work for us, but just like people use different things to protect their garden, we can use different means to protect our marriages –– as long as the goal is still the same.

Don't share deep personal stuff with a person you might be sexually attracted to. This is an expansion of something we said last week. This definition is a little fuzzy, so you will probably need to have a conversation to firm up what will work for you. For us, we don't ever meet alone with a person of the opposite gender and we don't have private conversations with them. Sometimes I need to send an e-mail to a woman or Andrea needs to call a man or something – we just tell each other that the conversation is going on and what happened. That way if anyone ever accuses one of us to the other we already know what's going on and why.

In public, talk about your spouse in positive ways. This can be difficult if you are around people who tend to spouse bash. It's common among people at work, comedians, friends, etc. But it is just a bad idea. Sure your spouse has problems, and sure you might need to talk to someone about them, but keep that conversation small and private. Don't advertise to the world that you are unhappy with your spouse. I'm not saying that you should be fake or disingenuous, just don't go into gory detail or say things that will make your spouse look like a terrible person. And, if possible, only share this stuff with people who will support you and your marriage so that when they hear your complaints (because we all have them), they won't encourage you to get a divorce, but to find ways to help your marriage grow.

Andrea & James T. Wood

Discussion:

What things have you found that help your marriage grow? What things tear it down? How could you set up barriers to the negative things?

What do you say when you hear people bashing marriage? What do you wish you could say?

Talk about the awkwardness of some of these boundaries (people will look at you weird when you tell them you can't do something "normal" because you're married). What will you do when an awkward situation comes up?

Week 19 – Boundaries with Friends

Boundaries help to minimize the potential for damage to your marriage through infidelity. A big part of the reason for not being alone with a person to whom you might be sexually attracted is to prevent situations where romantic feelings might start and grow. But it's natural to have a crush on someone every once in a while. I know that if you're a newlywed, you probably think that you will never even look at another person. The reality is that you will. You will see someone who is attractive to you and you will develop a crush on them. Crushes are like any thoughts, you can't control them, but it's your choice whether you act on them.

It's awkward to tell your spouse about a crush, but it's really the best choice. Both Andrea and I have had to do this a few times in our marriage. I can't think of anything that we've done that is more awkward, uncomfortable, weird and scary than having that conversation. I just want to stress that so you don't think that we're different or anything. We're not special, it's super weird. But it's also very much worth it.

Talking about it takes the power away. If you keep it a secret, then you might find reasons to be around that person. You might daydream about your crush. You might fantasize about what it would be like to be with them. But once you tell your spouse all the mystery and danger goes away. You see it for what it is – a Junior High School infatuation. This also gives your spouse the permission to defend you from potentially weird situations with the crushee. If you've been married over a year the odds are pretty high that at least one

Andrea & James T. Wood

of you has had a crush, don't hide from it; talk about it.

Discussion:

Talk about the first crush you had when you were growing up. What was it like? What was the result?

As you were dating what kind of people did you find attractive? What characteristics were common among them?

What could you do to make your marriage a safe enough place so that you could tell your spouse about a crush? What is your biggest fear in talking about crushes?

Week 20 – Boundaries with Personality

Boundaries are a positive thing we can do to provide space for healthy activity. A boundary around a playground allows the kiddos to have fun without fear of getting run over by a car. A boundary around a garden provides a way to keep pests out and the good stuff in. The problem is that we often think of boundaries as rules instead of making space for healthy activity. One of the main areas where boundaries are helpful is in handling personality differences.

You may have noticed that you and your spouse are different (shocking, I know). That's probably a part of what attracted you to them in the first place. It's a good idea to set some boundaries that will give space for each of you to express your own personality in healthy ways. For us, it's setting a night where I can be alone – I'm naturally an introvert, so I need some time to just be alone and quiet. Andrea is an extrovert, so she needs time with people. One of the best things for us is for Andrea to have a weekly activity she can go to with friends and leave me at home. But, that's just us. It's up to you to figure out what will suit your personalities and schedules.

Switch roles periodically to understand your spouse's position. If one of you normally takes the lead in a situation, switch it up and see what happens.

Andrea & James T. Wood

Discussion:

What things do you like to do that your spouse doesn't?

How much time do you need in a week to do your own thing? What happens when you don't get enough personal time? What if you get too much?

How can you create opportunities for understanding your spouse's personality and point of view?

Week 21 – Boundaries with Family

It is too easy to let your family get in the middle of your marriage. Having healthy boundaries with your families will go a long way to insulating your marriage from problems. Counselors talk about family of origin and family of origin issues. Your family of origin had its own dynamics and processes that were at work, and most of the time they were functional . But your spouse had a different set of dynamics in place that led to different results. If you've been married for more than fifteen minutes, you know this stuff.

The boundaries that we want to discuss are boundaries of involvement. When you get married, you start a new family; it's time to leave your family of origin out of your new relationship. You should be involved with your family of origin as much as you want, but don't share your arguments with them and don't ask them to join in your arguments. Having a mother-in-law mad at a daughter-in-law because she wouldn't cook her son's favorite meal is a waste of everyone's time and it doesn't accomplish anything.

Money and family are usually a bad combination. Don't loan money to your family and don't take loans from them. The proverb says: the borrower is slave to the lender. Dave Ramsey, a financial advice guy, says that it makes Thanksgiving dinner taste different when you get all tangled up with loans and your family. It is far better to not mix loans with family.

Andrea & James T. Wood

Discussion:

What ways do you remember your family of origin encouraging your marriage? How have they helped you to be better at being married?

What habits did you pick up from your family of origin that drive your spouse crazy?

Have you ever been in debt to a friend or family member? How did it feel to spend money around them? How would loans change the dynamic with your in-laws?

Vacations

Vacations can be a good time to relax and refresh, but too often they are full of stress and frustrations. People often come back from their vacation and feel like they need a vacation.

Week 22 – Permission to Vacation

Take your offered vacation time and use it. Americans are known for not taking their vacation time. For some people it's some kind of badge of honor to work hard, others think that their vacation time is some sort of savings account. Taking vacation time will make you a better worker and help your company. More importantly it shows your family that they are a priority over your work.

Do something to get away from your daily life and routine. Seeing your extended family or working around the house is not a vacation. I don't know why, but a lot of people take their vacations to visit family or complete projects. A vacation is supposed to provide rest, and unfortunately time with family is not usually relaxing. It's okay to take time for just yourselves and to not be obligated to always visit family.

Not every vacation needs to be a huge trip. If a vacation is supposed to provide a break from life, you don't need to wait a year between vacations. A daytrip to the zoo can be a vacation. An overnight stay at the beach can be a vacation. A long weekend or a camping trip can be a vacation.

Discussion:

What is your favorite vacation memory from your childhood? What about it makes it your favorite?

What is the worst vacation you've ever been on? Why was it terrible?

How would you change your vacation habits?

Week 23 – Not a Vacation from Manners

The stereotypical vacation is supposed to be an exercise in selfishness. TV and movies tell us that a vacation involves a waiter bringing you drinks while you sit by the pool or perhaps over-the-top adventures by land, sea, and air. The reality of vacations is far different, but we have this image drilled into us that on vacation all our wildest dreams will come true and we will be pampered in every way. That's a tough order to live up to!

You should divide responsibilities so that the necessary things get done. On vacation things still need to happen, plans need to be made, perhaps laundry needs to get done. No one person gets to be selfish and pampered at the expense of the other. Both of you are on vacation and both of you get to put in the work necessary to make the vacation good for both of you.

The goal is to create a situation where both of you can enjoy yourselves and relax. What that situation looks like may vary wildly, but you both need to be able to embrace the situation as a break from your routine and a time to reconnect with each other. You aren't taking a break from your manners when you're on vacation.

Discussion:

When you interact with people, what manners are the most important for you to see? To show?

Have you ever been on a vacation that was entirely focused on someone else? One entirely focused on you?

How do you think you could find a sense of balance between you and your spouse while on vacation?

Week 24 – Your Vacation Language

I don't know if you remember talking about love languages back in week 5, but we're going to apply that principle to vacation time. Andrea and I discovered, mostly through fighting, that we have different ideal vacations. Mine would involve very little planning and a lot of rest and relaxation. Good books and a comfy place to sit in a serene location are the elements of bliss for me. Andrea, on the other hand, wants to go and do and experience. She wants to plan each day of the vacation to pack in as much stuff as possible. For her, the ideal is to do things that she's never done and to go places that she's never been.

We learned that our ideas of vacation don't play very well together, especially if we are laboring under the assumption that vacation is a selfish endeavor. Some couples advocate taking separate vacations for this very reason, and while that might be fun on occasion, the majority of your vacations should be with your spouse. So, how do you solve this dilemma?

We have talked about this and we came to the conclusion that vacations need to be restful and rejuvenating. When you get back from vacation you want to feel invigorated and refreshed. My idea of vacation is the restful part, but it's not very rejuvenating. Andrea's idea of vacation is invigorating, but when it's over we need another vacation. So we are trying to do both in one trip so that we are both refreshed and rejuvenated. I think that most couples will have a relaxer and a doer; guess what, you both get a vacation.

Discussion:

What are your love languages (from week 5)? Do you think your love languages affect your vacation language?

We found that we both have exceptions to our ideal vacation where we would do the opposite (I would be super busy and Andrea would relax). What would cause you to make an exception to your ideal vacation?

Are there other vacation languages other than relaxation and rejuvenation?

Week 25 – Purposeful Adventure

Vacations don't always have to be about going to a tropical island and lying in the sun. Sometimes, it can be great to use your vacation time for a different reason. Some people use their paid time off to volunteer or to work on a project, and that can be just as rejuvenating as sitting on a beach. The important thing is that you and your spouse need to have the same purpose.

What things get the two of you excited? What really breaks your heart? Maybe you both love animals and you want to take time to volunteer at the humane society. The key for a purposeful vacation is the same as for other vacations; you need to be working together toward the same end. It won't work if just one of you wants to counsel at a camp, both of you need to be engaged and excited.

Having a purpose for your vacation time can transform what is normally a fleeting pleasure into a source of lasting satisfaction. The tan from the beach fades away quickly, but building a house or helping someone in need can provide joy for years.

Discussion:

What things would you both want to do with your time off? What causes really connect with you?

Have you ever used your time off to volunteer? What was the experience like?

What do you think is a fair amount of your time off to use for purposeful vacations? What amount needs to be reserved for rest and rejuvenation?

Purpose

It seems like the unspoken purpose for marriage is for people to be happy. I can't tell how many movies I've seen that have the general thesis: If two people love each other and make each other happy, they should get married. The problem with that idea is that happiness is fleeting and fickle. If happiness is the purpose of marriage, then marriages will fail when the happiness fades. But, if there's something bigger holding you and your spouse together, you can weather the storms of life.

Week 26 – "Normal" Marriages

If you're like us, then you got married because that's what you're supposed to do after you've been dating a while (and, if you are religious like we are, because you really wanted to have sex). It's sort of like the American dream, you date, you get married, you get jobs, you buy a house, you have children, you retire, have grandchildren, and then you die. We both grew up with this general plot-line in mind. But then something happened.

We were talking to an older couple and they were sharing about their marriage and their life together (they came up earlier, but their story applies here too). They had some difficult times that they were sharing and they said: "If our marriage didn't have a purpose we never would have made it through that time." We both were struck by that sentence, how could a marriage have a purpose? Isn't marriage basically just the next step in the plot? Marriage is supposed to make us happy (and let us have sex) and move us toward having children. How could marriage have a purpose beyond all of that?

Now, I want to make it very clear, the "normal" plot line for marriages is not bad. There is nothing wrong with doing exactly that. But what we discovered is that normal doesn't necessarily have any meaning (it can, but it doesn't have to). Don Miller wrote a book called *A Million Miles in a Thousand Years* in which he talks about making your life's story better. The normal marriage story is boring; there is no drive, no conflict, and no passion. What we're given as the story of marriage is "happily ever after" which is the end of the story, but marriage isn't static. It's a dynamic, moving, living thing that can never stay the same. It's either getting better or getting worse.

Discussion:

Growing up, what did you think life was supposed to look like? How has your life lined up with that vision or deviated from that vision?

Think about your favorite stories and movies. What makes them so good? What do the characters do to drive the story?

When you imagine the rest of your life, what does that look like? Would you want to read your story?

Week 27 – Finding Purpose

Since most marriages don't start with a clearly defined purpose, it's up to you to find the purpose for your marriage. But don't worry about coming up with some great idea that will carry you through without fail from here until you die. That's too much pressure to put on a short statement – think of a purpose more like a compass that helps you set a direction for your marriage. You always have the option of refining your direction, but if you don't start moving, knowing the right direction won't do you any good.

There are a few ways to work toward finding the purpose for your marriage. One way is to use the lottery question: If you won the lottery, what would you do? The answer to this question should give you some clues to what drives the two of you. Another way is to look at the stories that inspire you. What movies do you watch over and over? Do you like the happy endings? Do you love people that overcome adversity? The elements of the stories that inspire you may help you to discover your purpose.

Andrea and I tend to define purpose simply: it's something that lets you say, "no" when you need to. If your purpose is too vague or too specific it won't give you the ability to evaluate your decisions. A good purpose is general enough that it can encompass most circumstances in your lives, but it's pointed enough that it allows you to weed out decisions that aren't in line with your goals as a family.

Discussion:

Think about the worst corporate mission statements you've ever heard (or church mission statements). What makes them so terrible? How can you avoid that when you work on finding a purpose for your marriage?

If you were to label the purpose for your marriage up to this point, what would it be? Is there direction to your marriage?

What might prevent you from finding a purpose for your marriage? Have you ever known anyone who has identified and lived a purposeful marriage?

Week 28 – Implementing Purpose

Now that you have discovered your special purpose (a gold star for anyone who can name that reference), it's time to do something about it. Too many mission statements exist only on a piece of paper – if you went to all the trouble to work out a purpose for your marriage, you owe it to yourself and your spouse to put it into practice.

Start with small steps. If your purpose is to live debt free, you can't do that all at once. It takes a plan and patience to implement a purpose. The problem with most mission statements is that people usually forget about them within a month. The same is true of your marriage – if you don't have some system to remind yourselves of your purpose every few weeks, you'll forget and move on with life as usual. Revisit your purpose monthly to keep it fresh and find small ways you can live out your purpose each month.

For us a monthly goal sheet has been helpful. We have a few categories that we talk about (money, health, spirituality, emotions, and careers) and we've set yearly goals for each category. Each month we figure out what we can do to move toward our yearly goal. It's been a good way for us to keep our purpose on our minds.

Discussion:

Think about a time when you set goals that didn't work out. What was it that kept you from accomplishing the goals? How could you improve?

What goals could you set based on the purpose for your marriage? What steps can you take to reach those goals?

What things can you exclude from your life by living with purpose? How can a purpose make your life simpler?

Week 29 – Refining Purpose

The stories that captivate us are the ones where the characters change. The young boy grows into a brave man; the awkward girl grows into a captivating woman. We love stories about change, in part, because they remind us of the power of change. It is possible to be someone else, someone better. You aren't stuck like this.

Marriage is the same, or it should be. A great marriage will be different in the future. There's this myth that marriage should be locked in the bliss of the honeymoon (and I think that's why a lot of people get divorced). The truth is that a great marriage just keeps getting better. It gets better because both people are working on it and doing what they can to improve.

If you have a purpose for your marriage, you've gone beyond the majority of married couples, but you can't stop there. Regularly you should get together to check up on how your purpose is working out. Are you leaning toward one or two areas and neglecting others? That might be a sign that you should refine your purpose. It's a circular process, what you value defines what your purpose is and your purpose defines where you spend your time, effort and money, which helps you to value it more.

Discussion:

Describe the last time you had an annual review at work. Was it a positive or negative experience? What value do you see in the review process?

What things in your life have the ability to define your purpose (family, religion, etc.)? What things in your life are defined by your purpose? What's the difference between them in your marriage?

How frequently do you want to review your purpose?

Week 30 – Sharing Purpose

One of the main contributing factors to a successful marriage is having a shared purpose that is beyond either person. That means the shared purpose can't just be the desires of one spouse that the other person helps with, but it has to be a genuine passion for both people in the relationship. Couples with a shared purpose report more satisfaction with life and marriage than those without a shared purpose.

When you work together toward the same goals, you draw closer in every area of your relationship. Building a house together for charity, if you're both passionate about that cause, will give you a better sex life, financial unity and more fulfilling play. The reason is that you are creating long-term happiness that improves everything else.

Psychologists have determined that there are three main types of happiness: gratification, accomplishment and purpose. Gratification is when you eat a delicious meal, watch a funny movie or soak up sun on a gorgeous beach; the joy is immediate, but the feeling soon fades. Accomplishment is the feeling of working hard and producing something good; the happiness lasts longer, in part, because it took more effort to attain. Purpose is being committed to something that is greater than yourself and benefits other people to somehow make the world better; the joy of purpose lasts the longest, but it takes a long time to find. Sharing the greatest joy with your spouse will make accomplishments and gratifications even better as well.

Discussion:

How long does the joy of a gratification last for you? What about accomplishments?

Have you felt the happiness of a purposeful life? How is it different from the other two types of happiness?

What types of accomplishments have you shared as a couple? Does the sharing of happiness change the experience?

Money

Money is one of the most contentious issues in marriage. Dave Ramsey likes to say that money amplifies character, the more money gets involved, the more character traits will come out. Sure, the good traits will emerge, but so will the bad. In a marriage, this spells conflict.

Week 31 – Defining the Problem

Money fights are common ground in marriage. If you aren't fighting about money, you surely know a couple who is. It's not just fights about too little money. Lottery winners are generally a miserable bunch because too much money ruined their relationships. The odd thing is that there is never an amount of money that is just right. You can have too much or not enough, but the happy balance never arrives.

Money isn't bad, it's just a shorthand for trading goods and services. The problem is that money condenses all of that value down into a piece of paper or a number on a computer screen. For some reason that number can intoxicate people. We need to stop and realize that money is just a tool, it's a way for us to translate work into the stuff we need.

You need to know our bias. We've decided to live without debt. Unfortunately we didn't make that decision until after we already had some. We approach the money issue from that perspective. But, more important than how you choose to approach debt is how you approach money together. Our bias will come out in the following weeks, but the goal, for us, isn't to try to get you to agree with us, but to get you to agree with each other. Fights about money are the direct result of disagreements about money (crazy, I know), so if you take the time to work through the conflict, the fights will fade away.

Andrea & James T. Wood

Discussion:

When is the last time you fought about money? What was the issue? How did you resolve it?

Growing up how did money come into play? Were you rewarded for schoolwork with money? Did you have to work to earn your allowance? Did you have to get a job to help your parents pay the bills? How do you think that affects your attitude toward money now?

Week 32 – Budgets and Communication

Budgeting is probably the most helpful thing to do to get on the same page regarding money, but it's also a huge minefield of conflict. We need to let our budgeting be a way to have conversation rather than a way for us to try to control each other. What often happens is that there are two types of people. Dave Ramsey calls them the free spirit and the nerd. The free spirit likes to have fun and go to parties and go on vacation. The nerd likes to make lists and keep everything organized and situated. When it comes to money it often works out that the nerd becomes a parent to the free spirit and this makes the free spirit want to rebel.

Figure out who you are in the relationship. Marriages need nerds and free spirits. I'm a nerd; I like to make sure our bank account is nice and full. Andrea is the free spirit and she likes to make sure we aren't boring people. If it wasn't for Andrea I would be boring (so boring you don't want to know), and if it weren't for me, Andrea wouldn't know where her money was going. We need each other to be successful. We both have input into our budget so that it's organized and thoughtful and it allows us to have adventures at the same time.

Budgets may seem like a list of numbers (and they are), but what they really do is offer opportunities for communication. Work out your budget (go to DaveRamsey.com and look at his sample budget for a good idea) and then remember that you will need to revise this thing. You won't get it right the first time. For the first three or four months you will need to talk about your budget every month to tweak things to make sure that you have enough money for food and gas and vacations. Then you need to talk about your budget again every time your income or your expenses change. It's not as bad as it sounds, once you get it down it will go pretty smoothly, but those first few months will be a challenge. Stick with it and you will see great results.

Discussion:

What did you learn about budgeting from your parents? Do you follow what you learned from them?

Are you the nerd or the free spirit? How can you use your powers for good and not for evil?

Have you tried to write a budget as a couple before? How did it work out? Why? What problems do you have with budgeting?

Week 33 – Debt

We aren't fans of debt. In our marriage, we have been incredibly blessed to get out of debt and stay out of debt. But we don't want to force our opinions on you, if you don't want to jump on the Dave Ramsey bandwagon we can still be friends, and your marriage can still be fantastic. The real goal of getting out of debt is to feel peace about money and to have freedom to achieve your financial goals. It's possible to do those things without getting out of debt.

Debt creates stress and constraint. Stress because of the obligations you have to pay bills monthly and the constraint to be forced to use your money to service your debt instead of saving for the things you really want to do. A lot of people will tell you that you need debt, that debt is a good thing, because it allows you to build a credit score. The truth is that a credit score is just a measure of how well you handle debt; if you don't want to borrow money you don't need good credit. And, if you want to buy a house, you can still find banks that will manually underwrite your loan, meaning that they will look at your income and assets to determine your ability to pay, not just rendering judgment based on a number in a computer system.

All that aside, the point of this conversation is for you and your spouse to figure out, together, how you can reduce stress and constraint in your budget so that you can have peace and freedom. When it comes down to it, the stress and constraint we feel in our budgets have a lot to do with the fights we have over money. Your arguments about money will drastically decrease when the monthly bills don't stress you out and you don't feel trapped when you look at your bank statement.

Discussion:

If you have debt, have you considered that you might not need it? What would your life look like without any debt but your house? What if you paid off your house early? What could you do with your money then?

What are the major causes of stress when it comes to your budget? How would you feel if you woke up and you didn't have any debt? Would it reduce your stress?

What goals do you have for your finances? Can you achieve those goals now or is something constraining your use of money?

Week 34 – Money and Goals

Money is a tool we can use to help us achieve our goals. Remember the purpose and goals that you set for your life and your marriage. Money is one of the ways you can move closer to those goals, it's not the only way to achieve your goals, but it can help.

One goal is to live a fulfilling life, make memories and enjoy the present. Don't save for the future at the expense of the present. It can be tempting to put away every penny for the future and to not enjoy life now. That is as wasteful as being in massive debt. Constantly putting off the goals in your marriage until some vague future date so that you can save more money is a waste of the time you have now. Sacrifice is good, to an extent. Saving money is good. Avoiding debt is good. But don't overdo the good things to the point that they prevent you from living life now.

Discussion:

What things can you do now to move toward your long-term goals?

How can you creatively achieve your goals for less or no money? Could you travel in a less expensive way (backpack, work your way around the world, etc.)? Could you create family memories by doing things that are cheap or free? Could you trade or volunteer?

How is money a tool that is helping you? How is money preventing you from achieving your goals?

Holidays

Holidays can be a large source of stress. You can feel pulled in a thousand different directions and it seems like there's no right choice. It doesn't have to be a struggle every year, but it will take some discussion to come together around the holidays.

Week 35 - Dealing with Family

Our families of origin are usually the main source of pressure around the holidays. They can offer pressure directly through requests to be with them during the holidays, and they can offer indirect pressure through comments about holiday activities. It's important to fairly balance your time with your families, but remember fair, not necessarily equitable. You don't have to spend the exact same amount of time with each family, but an appropriate amount of time.

Don't forget when you're balancing families that your new family counts. As a married couple your top priority is to your new family, and after that to your families of origin. Do what's best for your family, not your families of origin. If at all possible you should keep the peace with your original families and you should spend time with them as you want, but don't neglect your new family for the sake of your original families.

Set clear boundaries for your original families. If you decide that you'll swap Thanksgiving and Christmas every other year, then stick to that and don't let your original families pressure you to change. It's important that they know your new family is separate from them (though you are connected). They no longer have the right to tell you what to do, they can only invite and request.

Discussion:

Discuss the pressures you feel from your family of origin around the holidays. How can you support your spouse when they feel those pressures?

Are there situations where your family of origin doesn't respect your new family's boundaries? How can you communicate your boundaries to them in a loving way?

How could you creatively organize your holidays to include both your families?

Week 36 - Creating Your Own Traditions

Find ways to set your new family apart from your original family. For us we decided to spend our first set of holidays away from everyone. We stayed home and enjoyed our own time together. We figured that we would offend everyone equally in order to be fair to everyone. Since then we've been free to join with our families on our terms, not theirs.

Take the best of both original families to create your new traditions. Some of our original family traditions are really good, some not so much. Find the good and get rid of the bad. Don't feel like you need to recreate one set of traditions, the goal is for you to blend together and create something new that is unique to your family.

Traditions are good to help connect us to our past, but they don't have to be followed blindly. Traditions are just a tool that we can use to build good marriages and families – there's nothing sacred about traditions, unless you want to make them sacred. You may decide to not give gifts in your family one year in order to spend time looking at consumerism as a family – that doesn't mean you have to stop giving gifts for all time, just that you took a break for a while. Let traditions do what they were meant to do, but not more than that.

Andrea & James T. Wood

Discussion:

What traditions from your family of origin were good? What traditions annoyed you? Which ones are worth keeping?

What traditions do you wish you had growing up? Does your spouse's family have any of those traditions? How can you learn from each other?

What do your traditions remind you of? Do you need to stop traditions, continue them, or change them?

Week 37 - Planning ahead

Sometimes holidays can sneak up on you. You'd think that they wouldn't, since they rarely change their schedules, but somehow life gets going and those holidays creep up. Then, without warning it's time for a birthday or Thanksgiving or something. Take some time to work out your schedule ahead of time – maybe a month in advance or even longer. It can be helpful to save up your money a little bit at a time for gifts or trips so you don't feel pressured when the expenses come around.

Decide what your plans are before the big day arrives. If you are working on Christmas plans, then set them at least a month in advance so you don't have competing expectations when the day rolls around. We've always found that we tend to forget about plans for New Year's Eve with all the focus on Christmas. Sitting down ahead of time helps you to avoid arguments in the midst of the holidays. There's enough stress as it is so be sure to plan ahead.

Don't forget about those other holidays such as birthdays, Valentine's Day, and Arbor Day (if that's a big deal to you). A lot of focus and energy goes to the holidays from Thanksgiving through New Year's so it can seem like the others are less important. It is helpful to build expectation and anticipation for all the important days in the year. Be sure that you are working together toward a mutual appreciation of the holidays rather than just using one person's opinion as the standard.

Andrea & James T. Wood

Discussion:

What has been your experience with under planned (or over planned) holidays? How has that affected your ability to enjoy the holiday?

Create a top five list of holidays; compare your list with your spouse's. What is your ideal way to celebrate each holiday?

How important were birthdays in your original family? Do you want to continue those traditions or start new birthday traditions with your spouse?

Week 38 - Purposeful Holidays

Often holidays are a family focused time, but it's good to remember other people too. This doesn't have to be an either/or issue. Sometimes I've felt pressured like I need to spend all of my time over the holidays feeling guilty. But there are great programs like the Advent Conspiracy that encourage people to give one less present and then give that extra money away to help people. You can still enjoy your holiday and have a higher purpose for things.

You might share your holiday time with people who are alone, like college students or people living away from their families. Use your holiday party or meal to share with those who might be alone otherwise. Make sure that you are inviting people as a couple rather than just one person being involved in the process. Decide together how you can share your holidays.

Also remember that you are both responsible for whatever you add to your holiday. If you decide to welcome more people into your home for Thanksgiving dinner it's not just up to the cook to feed twice as many people. Both of you need to address the added work. Or if you decide to help build a house for charity, it's not just up to the home-repair person to do the work. Doing these things together is as important and what you choose to do.

Andrea & James T. Wood

Discussion:

Have you ever spent time doing charity work over the holidays? How did you like it? How did it make you feel?

How could a purposeful holiday tradition encourage your family and your marriage? What can you do to avoid discouragement through the holidays?

If you came up with a purpose for your marriage (remember week 27?), how could you use that to infuse your holidays with purpose?

Week 39 – Realistic Expectations

Norman Rockwell doesn't live at your house. Sometimes we think he should, but the truth is that none of us have that "perfect" experience over the holidays. The problem is that we can increase our stress and the conflict in our marriage when we put unrealistic expectations on our holidays.

Enjoy what you have, not what you think you ought to have. We live in a consumer-driven, materialistic world, so it's difficult to not want more. We're trained to want more, but we can never appreciate what we want. We can only appreciate what we have. We already talked about not living in the past with the traditions of our original families, but we need to make sure that we're not living in our wants or comparison to other people. We need to make sure that we're not living in the future with our expectations of what holiday memories we will create.

Often the best holiday memories and traditions come about unexpectedly. One of our favorite memories came from our first Christmas when I was attending graduate school in Memphis. We were too poor to buy a tree so I took green construction paper and cut out a tree that we could put on our table. We still have it and bring it out every year. We didn't plan to be so poor, but the memory and experience are invaluable.

Andrea & James T. Wood

Discussion:

Talk about a time when you were disappointed over a holiday when you were growing up. How did you feel? What caused your disappointment?

Have you had unexpected surprises over the holidays that turned out enjoyable? What helped you to appreciate the unexpected?

Discuss what your expectations are before the holidays arrive (now might be a good time). What expectations can you let go? What one or two expectations that you have are the most important to you?

Children

Choosing to have kids and how to raise them has a big impact on marriage. We asked several couples in different stages of marriage and parenting to share with us their thoughts and experiences. These conversations aren't about how to be a better parent, but how to be a better spouse with kids around.

Week 40 - Deciding Whether or Not to Have Kids and When

It may sound weird to have a week devoted to the decision to have kids. When we got married we assumed that we would be having kids eventually. We just thought that was the natural course of events, but we ended up meeting a few couples who had decided that they weren't called to be parents and it opened up the possibility to us. Remember, it's your decision, it's not your friends' or your parents' decision.

When deciding whether or not to have kids, you should look at what will be the best for the children. Often, it seems, the decision to have kids is driven by happiness. To make the parents happy or the grandparents or just about anyone else. It's a sacrifice to have kids. The research shows that marital satisfaction decreases when you have children. This doesn't mean that the marriages are worse, but satisfaction decreases. Make sure you're willing to sacrifice your own short-term happiness for the sake of your children (the marital satisfaction does increase after the kids leave home).

We realize that you may already have kids at this point in your marriage. We're not trying to say you should go back and do it over. Start where you are and look at how the children are affecting your marriage. Children transform marriage so it's important to use these principles going forward.

Finally, we just need to clarify that the decision on whether or not to have children must be a mutual one. No one person has the right to decide for both of you.

Discussion:

Have you felt pressured to have kids? How did that make you feel?

How do you think children challenge a marriage? How do they help a marriage?

Think about a time that you had to make a difficult decision. How did you come to a resolution? Was that a good experience or a bad experience?

Week 41 – Preparing to Parent

Since we don't have children we wanted to get some additional input for this part of the challenge. We surveyed several parents that we know regarding how having children has affected their marriage. The following weeks will be a synthesis of their responses (not the responses of any one family) along with our research.

We asked the following questions:
How does having children affect your marriage? What has been the most challenging?

How do you find time to be together as a couple with children around? What do your dates look like?

As a couple, how have you worked out parenting styles? What was the conversation like between the two of you regarding this decision?

From that we want to look at three phases of parenting and how they affect marriage. Preparation, adjustment, and stabilization. Preparing starts at pregnancy and with each new stage of your children's lives you'll need to prepare together. It's important that you try to have conversations about dating, parenting styles, vacations, and everything else before they become an issue. That doesn't mean that you'll anticipate everything (or even most things), but by working to prepare, you strengthen your marriage and become unified as parents.

Probably my favorite statement from all of our surveys is:

"Having children is awesome and terrible!" I think that sums it up beautifully. Children are able to look at you and smile or giggle and make you feel like the best person in the world. They are also able to look at you and start crying and make you feel like the worst person in the world. The idea is to help each other balance out the awesome and the terrible. Get to know the warning signs in your spouse and your kids that indicate a swing from awesome to terrible and do your best to intervene. It will take practice, but you can help each other have more awesome than terrible if you prepare for it.

Take time when you're not feeling stressed and ready to strangle kids to have some conversations about your relationship and your priorities. Think about what will allow you to communicate your love and respect to each other even in the most stressful and tiring situations. Since stress and tiredness increase the likelihood of conflict it's probably best to try to have these conversations at low-stress, well-rested times.

Andrea & James T. Wood

Discussion:

When you prepare for a trip which one of you is the organizer (you know, with the check-list) and which one of you is the last-minute packer? How does that affect your relationship? How do you think those styles affect your relationship as you parent?

Think of a time when you knew what your spouse wanted without them having to say anything. What clued you in to their feelings? How can you learn more cues about your spouse's emotions?

Discuss what is most important to you about your relationship with your spouse (think about your love languages and the purpose for your marriage). If there was only one thing your spouse could do each week to communicate their love for you, what would it be?

Week 42 – Adjusting to Parenting

Having children is a significant adjustment, and moving from one child to two is nearly as large an adjustment as becoming parents for the first time. It's important to remember that adjusting your marriage to having kids is a continual process. You won't just figure it out one time and then have it all worked out, you'll need to continue to adjust and change your habits to find what works for you and your spouse. One of the key things that we've learned in all our interviews is that you need to find what works best for your family. Experiment, converse, and explore.

It's difficult to separate parenting from the marriage relationship. This is good and bad. The good part is that the increased need for communication and patience when dealing with children can make your marriage relationship better. The accountability of knowing that the marriage that you model is the example of marriage that will have the greatest impact on your children can encourage a better marriage, even when it's difficult.

The bad part of marriage and parenting being so intertwined is that you can lose perspective on the marriage due to the demands of parenting. The needs of children are urgent: they cry, they complain, they whine and sometimes throw fits if they don't get what they want. Your spouse may say nothing when they need you. It takes a special effort to see what your spouse needs in the midst of the urgent demands of your children.

Andrea & James T. Wood

Discussion:

What was the greatest adjustment you made when you first got married? How did you work through the process together? What processes can you put in place to keep adjusting to kids?

What impact did your parent's marriage have on yours? Do you find yourself emulating them or trying to be different? How do you want to impact your children?

What unique communication do you have with your spouse? What inside jokes and meaningful looks do you share? How can you maintain communication in the midst of parenting?

Week 43 – Rhythms of Parenting

Avoid becoming strangers. Too often married couples get to the point where their kids are leaving the house only to find that they don't know each other. With the competing, urgent demands of raising children and working jobs, the important work of staying connected to your spouse can be neglected. If you aren't intentional about creating time to spend with your spouse you won't eventually find the time. In order to say 'yes' to your marriage you need to say "no' to something else to make time.

Develop age appropriate rhythms with your children. You may not be able to have your 2 year old sit for an hour while you and your spouse reconnect, but you can probably get them to sit quietly for a couple minutes so you can spend some quality time with your spouse. It's important to not just wait until the kids fall asleep to have time together daily. Your children need to see how important your marriage is, and the two of you need to have the energy to enjoy your time together. As your children get older you can find more time together, maybe first thing in the morning over coffee or right as you get home from work.

Create daily, weekly, monthly and annual rhythms. A few minutes together every day helps to maintain the connection, but to keep growing in your marriage you need to spend time in larger chunks. Every week you should set aside some time together (maybe to have a conversation about how to improve your marriage). If you have young, kids you might not be able to get out for a date once a week, but setting aside time, even if it's at home, is important.

Andrea & James T. Wood

Also look at monthly and yearly activities that you can make a part of your life for the sake of your marriage.

Discussion:

Talk about a friend that you have lost touch with. What allowed the friendship to work? What caused you to drift apart?

How can you find ways to connect in five minutes? Could you play a game where you each get to ask one question? Should you just sit and hold hands?

When do you have time every day to spend with your spouse? Every week? Every month? How can you re-organize your schedule to make time together?

Rhythm and Blues

There are natural rhythms to life and marriage, some of which are good, and some make us sad. Taking into account and planning for both the good and the bad in life helps to make marriage more enjoyable, but also more resistant to struggle.

Week 44 – Stress and Release

The natural rhythm to life is to gear up for a goal and then relax afterward. Think about a school schedule – we work hard toward a goal and then we take a break. Our lives move in this rhythm for the first two decades, and it becomes ingrained in us. In fact, this is how we function well. Even our daily and weekly schedules show a period of activity and a period of rest.

Stress and release are both necessary parts of life; we can't have only one or only the other. For some reason we've gotten the message that when we grow up and get a "real job"" we are supposed to move constantly toward the next goal (i.e. stay in a state of constant stress) until we get to relax through retirement. All stress for decades and then all release until we die. The truth is that the healthiest people in the world enjoy both times of stress and release so that they have a balance in their lives.

Every marriage has an example of this process: planning a wedding is incredibly stressful and then the honeymoon is a time to relax and enjoy each other. We take a marriage retreat every year, which is usually a little stressful, so a week or two later we take a trip to celebrate. You can work hard toward the goal of paying off debt and then have a party to celebrate what you achieved. You can even relax after failing to meet a goal because you recognize that you worked toward something. A marriage without goals and rest can seem like a hamster wheel that spins until you die.

Andrea & James T. Wood

Discussion:

Think about a time that you've celebrated a successful goal. How important was the celebration and relaxation (if any) to feeling good about the goal?

Have you ever reached a goal but not had the opportunity to enjoy it? How does it feel to not have an opportunity to relax?

What goals do you have right now? How can you celebrate the completion of those goals? What natural rhythms can help with this process (e.g. children's school schedule)?

Week 45 - Dealing with Loss During the Holidays

Holidays are a time of joy and celebration, but they also bring to mind the people that we've lost or the events that have caused us pain in the past. We grieve loss in different ways and for different things, but for some reason that loss comes out strongly during the holidays. Your spouse may not be the best person to talk to about this, even though they love you, they may not be able to help you through this situation.

Set up appropriate times and places to release the feelings of loss. Don't try to pretend like you haven't suffered a loss. You may need to spend time with a counselor talking through your grief. There is no weakness in asking for help. You don't think someone is weak if they go to a doctor when they're sick, so you shouldn't think someone is weak for seeking a counselor for help through grief.

Incorporate the joy of the person or thing you lost into your new holiday memories. Share stories with each other about how they made your holidays special. Don't dwell on the loss itself, but remember the impact they made on your lives. Find a balance that works well for you where you spend time recognizing the good of the past and how that shapes your holidays now.

Andrea & James T. Wood

Discussion:

What things do you grieve? Is it a lost parent or a house that burned down or a job that was lost?

What holiday traditions remind you of someone you've lost? Which holidays are especially important to you?

How do you deal with loss? How is that different from the way your spouse deals with loss? Are there ways you can grieve together? Are there ways you need to grieve separately?

What is the best way to honor the life of the person you lost?

Week 46 – Balance

We need to have up times and down times to have a healthy balance in our lives and marriages. Up time is time where you feel pressure to perform – this might be at work or school where you feel the pressure to do well at your job, or it might be in social situations where you feel the pressure to be accepted. Down times are the low or no pressure situations where you don't have to perform in any way, you can just be yourself. Our marriages need both. We need to, in a healthy way, feel the need to perform for each other and with each other for other people. We also need to have healthy ways to be down and not have pressure with each other or with other people.

This balance will look different for each individual and each couple. We need different amounts of up time and down time and we do different things with our up time and down time. One person might feel the need to perform on a hiking trip (they need to go a certain pace or look a certain way) where for another person, getting out and hiking lets them be completely down. It will take time to learn each other and the dynamic of your relationship to find the balance here.

Certain times of year have a lot of up time, all in a row. It's important for you to set boundaries and communicate well as the pressure to perform rises. Plan for and help each other find the down time necessary to have balance.

Andrea & James T. Wood

Discussion:

What situations make you feel like you need to perform? How is that a good thing? How is that a bad thing? What situations make you feel like you can just be yourself? How is that good? Bad?

Think about the last time you had to be up for your spouse. What was the occasion? How did it make you feel? How did it make your spouse feel? What is the ratio of up time to down time between you and your spouse?

How can you provide down time in the midst of the rush and bustle? How much down time do you think you need to feel well and balanced? How realistic is that?

Week 47 – Margin

Margin is the space at the edges of your life where you can incorporate the things you can't plan. When you have margin you have the ability to go out to dinner with your spouse when you find an old gift card. You can accept an invitation to volunteer together at the local charity. You can jump in the car and head to the coast for the day. Most of us idealize spontaneity and then we proceed to fill our lives with so many scheduled events that we don't have room for a spontaneous adventure. Your first step is to reduce your scheduled obligations.

You can create margin in your life through good planning. Tight scheduling kills margin. When you jump from one activity to another to another without any breaks in between all of the space is pushed out of your lives. Rather than try to squeeze as much stuff into your calendar as possible, plan to do things well. Don't schedule a dinner, a Skype call and a meeting all on the same night. Reserve your time for one or two things with a buffer in between. Also develop boundaries – if you have scheduled a night off, put it on your calendar and don't let anyone convince you to reschedule. If you have a date scheduled with your spouse, that time should be reserved for just the two of you. Healthy boundaries will create healthy margin.

The point of having margin in your marriage is to provide space for the joy of marriage in the midst of the work of marriage. Marriage is hard work, but we're willing to do the hard work because of the love we feel and the joy we share. But when our schedules get so tight that we don't have any room for fun, we lose the reason we're working so hard on marriage to begin with. Develop margin to give yourselves space to enjoy each other again.

Discussion:

Think about the last time that something unexpected came up in your life (good or bad). Did you have space for it? How did it affect your marriage?

Marriages usually have a planning-nerd and a spontaneous free-spirit. Which one are you? How does it make you feel when your preferences are not addressed?

You have to say: 'no' to some things in order to have space to say: 'yes' to other things. To what things do you need to say: 'no'? To what things would you like to be able to say: 'yes'?

Ask your spouse what benefits they expect or hope to get from increasing margin in your lives.

How to Encourage Other Marriages

It's all well and good for you to have a healthy, happy marriage, and that is where you need to start. But once you start figuring out a few things, you need to encourage other marriages. Take what you've learned and share it with other people, we all know you're not perfect and your marriage isn't perfect (neither is ours). Together we can help to make each other a little bit better and to make marriage better. A movement has to start somewhere. Is it with you?

Week 48 – Transparent Marriage

Share the good and bad in your marriage. For some reason we are conditioned as a culture to only share the good things that are going on in our lives. We share the job promotion, but we hesitate to mention the job loss. We talk about when the kids are doing well, but we don't mention when they're diagnosed with a learning disability. We brag on our recent cruise, but we don't talk about how we're in debt and desperate for money. What if we started sharing both the good and the bad things that are happening in our lives? It might give others the comfort to do the same.

Learn to fight in public. This is a tough one since fighting makes everyone nervous. We don't want to admit that we fight let alone show the world what it looks like. But what if we did? What if we learned how to disagree and work through our conflict in the line at the grocery store or in the lobby at church? The standard operating procedure is to avoid it, but what if we could model how healthy conflict looks where others can see it?

Be honest and open with your friends. If anyone deserves to know how you are really doing, it's your friends. When things are fantastic and joyful, share it with your friends. But when things are dark and dreary we tend to shut down and avoid "burdening"" our friends with our problems. You weren't made to work through things alone – even your marriage isn't supposed to stand alone. You are supposed to be surrounded by a community of support – but they can't support you without knowing what's going on.

Andrea & James T. Wood

In none of this am I suggesting that you should bad-mouth your spouse in public or private or use a public setting to get your way in conflict. You, as a couple, need to decide to live a transparent marriage and decide what things will be available to the public. This must be a mutual decision.

Discussion:

When is the last time you shared something good about your marriage in a public setting? When is the last time you shared a struggle? What's the difference? Why is our culture averse to sharing negative things?

How did you learn to have conflict with your spouse? What examples have you seen of marital conflict? How would it have changed things for you to see more examples of healthy marital conflict?

How would you respond if your friends shared their problems with you? Would you reject them or be ashamed of them? Why is it different for you sharing your problems?

Week 49 – Marriage Mentoring

Find older couples who can share with you how to have a healthy, long-lasting marriage. There are formal marriage mentoring programs that you can work with, or you can just find a couple that has the kind of marriage you want to have when you grow up. It's probably best that you don't choose someone too close to you – either of your parents would not be a good choice since you probably can't be totally honest with them. Rather find an older couple at church or maybe older cousins that have a healthy marriage and see if they would be willing to meet with you.

Learn the techniques of marriage mentoring. Marriage mentoring is really about conversation. It doesn't require much of the mentors or the mentees other than getting together on a regular basis to talk about marriage. The "Marriage Mentoring"" series put out by Dr. Ed Gray offers twelve conversations – one for each month – to guide the talk about marriage. You need to show up with a topic in mind (kids, finances, holidays, etc.) and then talk about it. Set the rules that nothing will be repeated outside the mentoring relationship and that no question is off limits.

Offer to mentor couples earlier in their marriage. Just because you haven't been married for 57 years doesn't mean you can't offer good advice and support to other couples. If you've been married for even a few years, you have something to offer to couples who are just about to be married or are just married. In fact you might be the best resource for them since the memory of being newly married is still fresh for you.

Discussion:

What marriages do you want to emulate? How do you find yourself imitating other marriages? Discuss the top three couples you would ask to mentor you.

How have you been helped by a mentor in the past? What setting helps you to share with a mentor; to learn from a mentor? How are you and your spouse different?

Who do you know that might need someone to talk to them about marriage? What younger couples are just married or just getting married? How do you think you could approach them to talk about marriage mentoring?

Week 50 – Double Dates

Spend time with other married couples to have fun and encourage each other. So much of our lives are built around work in all its forms. We need to have fun and we need to have fun with other people. A double date can be as simple as going to dinner or playing cards, but it gives you the chance to talk, joke, laugh, and encourage each other. You should absolutely date your spouse alone, but some of your dates should be with other couples.

Having fun together is a great way to encourage marriage. Showing and being shown how to have fun is an important exercise. I'm not suggesting that anyone doesn't know how to have fun, but sometimes we forget. Sometimes we get wrapped up in the busyness of life and we lose sight of the joy that exists. Getting together for a silly movie or a game of charades with another couple can renew your enthusiasm and breathe a breath of fresh air into both marriages. Seeing another couple enjoying life can remind you and your spouse to enjoy yours as well.

Discussion:

When is the last time you got together for a double date? What was good about it? What wasn't good?

Discuss the time you've spent with other couples. How has your marriage been affected? How do you think you affected the other marriage?

Week 51 – People are Different

It can be incredibly helpful to talk about your marriage to someone you aren't actually married to. But it can also be dangerous.

The dangerous side comes when you end up talking badly about your spouse, especially in situations where the person you're talking to might be attracted to you (or you might be attracted to them).

As a general rule, don't say mean stuff about your partner. It doesn't really help things. But sometimes you need to share frustrations with like-minded peers. That's okay, and helpful even, but not just getting together with people to reinforce negative feelings.

Think about your peer-group as a place where you can find sympathy, empathy and support for what you're dealing with. They might be able to offer some advice, or just sit with you as things are difficult (both are helpful). The overall goal of sharing about your relationship with your peers is to learn to understand your spouse better. Different perspectives and voices can give you a better approach to the same problem. The classic definition of insanity is doing the same thing repeatedly and expecting different results. If you're starting to feel a little bit insane in your relationship, it might help to try something different — like talking to people.

Discussion:

When was the last time you talked with your peers about your marriage? Was it helpful? What things could you talk about with that group that you wouldn't discuss in a mixed group?

Discuss the difference between honest dialog and badmouthing. Where is the line for you and your spouse?

Week 52 – Marriage Review

To end this year of conversation it will be good to look back at your marriage over the last twelve months to see what has changed (or what you wish had changed). Take a few minutes to think about the state of your marriage now. What do you like? What still frustrates you? What surprises you? What delights you? What disappoints you? Write down your thoughts and have your spouse do the same. Talk through your responses.

Take some time to look at how your marriage was a year ago. Get out the paper you wrote at the beginning of the Marriage Challenge. Talk about your answers to the questions: What were your major arguments? What made you happy? What did you never expect to change? What hopes did you have for the future of your marriage? Write down your responses and discuss them.

Finally talk about the change you've witnessed in your marriage. Has all of the change been for good? Are there changes you expected but didn't see? Are there changes you didn't expect but are happy to see? If you had it to do all over again what would you do differently? Write down and discuss your thoughts.

Hold on to the pages with your thoughts and look at them next year to spark some more discussion.

Bibliography

Chapman, G. D. (2010). *The 5 Love Languages: The Secret to Love That Lasts* (New Edition.). Northfield Publishing.

Cloud, H., & Townsend, J. (1992). *Boundaries: When to Say YES, When to Say NO, To Take Control of Your Life* (Revised.). Zondervan.

Eggerichs, E. (2004). *Love & Respect: The Love She Most Desires; The Respect He Desperately Needs* (1st ed.). Thomas Nelson.

Fisher, R., Ury, W. L., & Patton, B. (2011). *Getting to Yes: Negotiating Agreement Without Giving In* (Upd Rev.). Penguin (Non-Classics).

Gray, E. (2009). *12 Conversations.* 12conversations.com

Miller, D. (2011). *A Million Miles in a Thousand Years: How I Learned to Live a Better Story.* Thomas Nelson.

Wecks, E. (2012). *How to Manage Your Money When You Don't Have Any.* Wecks Publishing.

Smalley, D. G., & Trent, D. J. (2001). *Love Is A Decision.* Thomas Nelson.

About The Authors

James and Andrea Wood have been married since 2003. Since getting married they've lived in Oregon, Tennessee, Montana, California, Ireland, Hawaii and Washington. Travel, adventure and sharing what they've learned about how to have a fantastic marriage wake them up in the morning. James is a writer, speaker and blogger who has shared with audiences around the world. Andrea is a well-rounded person who loves mentoring people.

Connect with Us

This book is independently published, so we have no one but you to spread the word for us. If you liked this book and if it helped your relationship, consider giving us a good review on Amazon.com, "like" us on Facebook and tell your friends about how great the book is. You don't have to purchase the book on Amazon to leave a review. Just find the book listing (or click here if you have a digital copy) and scroll to the bottom of the page; click "Create Your Own Review" and say nice things about the book (careful or we'll blush).

Like us on Facebook at The Marriage Challenge page (tinyurl.com/MarriageChallenge).

Connect with James online:
Website - jamestwood.com

Email - me@jamestwood.com

Amazon.com - /James-T-Wood/e/B006RBPJZC

Twitter - @jtw78

Facebook - /jamestwood